ZEPHYR

SURYANSH S. CHAUHAN

Copyright © Suryansh S. Chauhan
All Rights Reserved.

ISBN 979-888629073-8

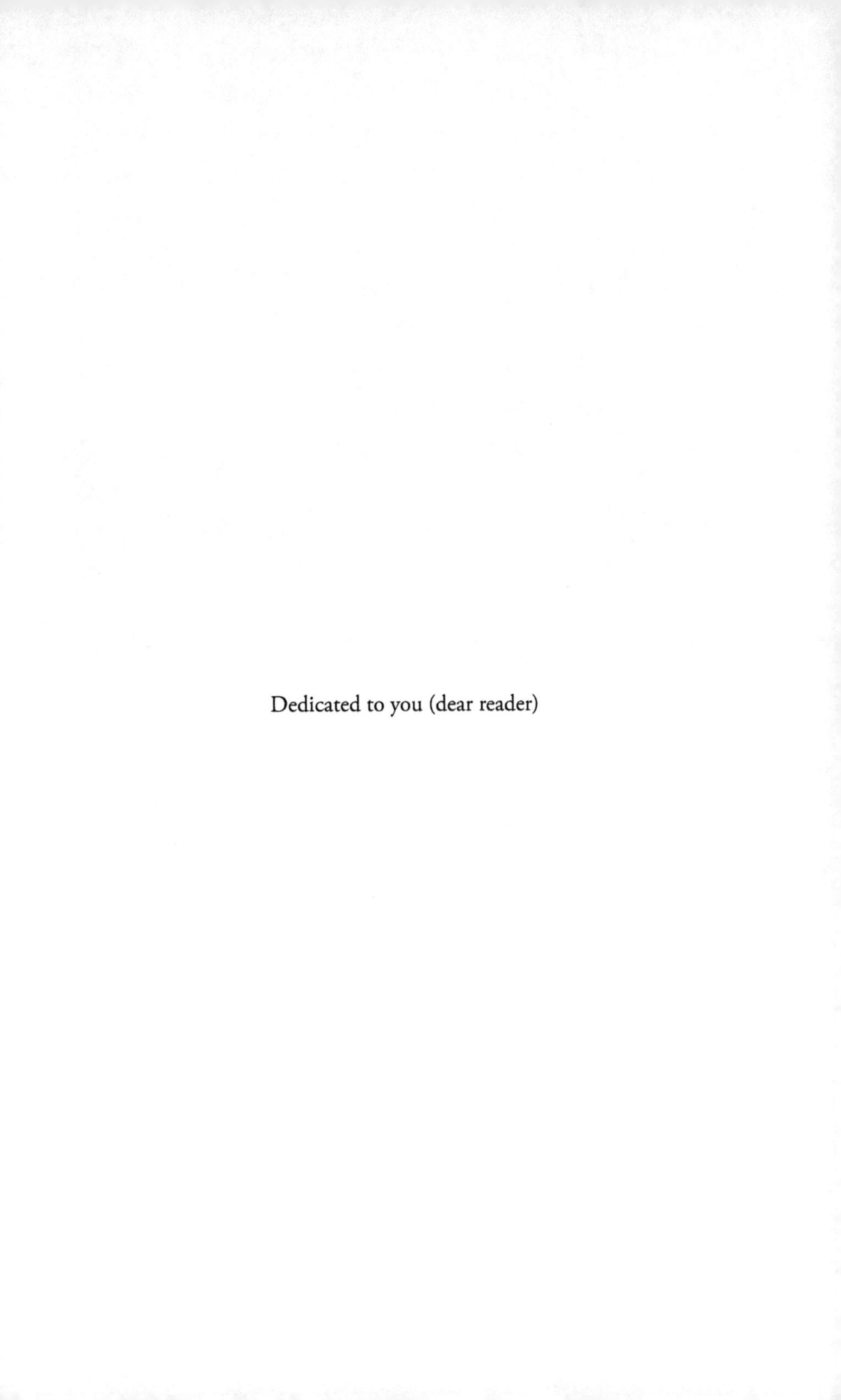

Dedicated to you (dear reader)

Contents

Contents

Contents

Copyright Disclaimer

This anthology is a work of fiction. All the poems and other write-ups are the original products of the co-authors are the products of the co-authors's imagination. Our editors have tried their best to check plagiarism in the content of all co-authors.

In case of any plagiarism, the co-author is solely responsible, and not the compiler or the publisher.

Preface

This is my 3rd anthology as a compiler and I'm really looking forward to it.

Acknowledgements

The successful compilation of this anthology would not have been possible without the hardwork and efforts of all the co-authors.

All the people involved in making of this anthology have devoted their time and energy for the success of the anthology.

I would like to thank my parents especially my mom from whom I inherited this skill and all my beloved friends, juniors and seniors for their constant support.

Prologue

Zephyr

A soft gentle breeze,
Brushing off against my face.
    Wind with different flavours,
Fragrance of land & seas.
    Such is the beauty of nature,
Loaded with diversity.
    Zephyr in my heart,
My soul is calm now.
    And the only place i wanna be at,
Is the azure sky where I can be free.
    I rejoice these moments,
When i feel alive.
    Like a bird,
Spreading its wings...
    In order to fly.
    ~Suryansh S. Chauhan (Compiler & Editor)

1. Suryansh S. Chauhan

Suryansh Chauhan (going by the pen name : Suryansh S. Chauhan) hails from the city of Gwalior, Madhya Pradesh (Born : 29th May, 2004).

This teenager is a student at DAV Kota. Apart from writing, he also has a great deal of interest in painting and photography. He's also a national level karate player & YouTuber for fun.

He started writing at the age of 14 and got published as a co-author at the age of 15 and then as a solo author at the age of 16. He believes that writing is all about framing one's own feelings, emotions or imagination in a way that it brings a sense of peace.

A lot of his poems are pretty long, simple and explanatory as if they're almost a song. He writes to express; for relief. Because he believes that art in any form is a therapy in itself.

Social Media—
Instagram : @suryansh_s_chauhan &
@thefadingbud_
Twitter : @Surya_S_Chauhan
Youtube : Suryansh S Chauhan
Mail : surya29.sc@gmail.com

We

The urge to be with you all the time,
Hug you tightly in my arms...

Isn't it weird,
We were almost strangers a while ago

Now madly in love.

Endless conversations,
Without any topic.

I feel like I'm me with you,
You opened my bottled up emotions.

No matter where you go
Or how much you change...

You'll always be an important chapter
In my story.

Isn't it weird,
How neither of us imagined...

That we'd be so much
Important to each other.

An unexpected love story,
Blooms before the spring...

Before most of the stories will end,
And many new will begin.

Weird, isn't it the right word?
Or maybe I should say...

A unique one,
That starts with you and me...
And hopefully ends with "we".

Imagination

Constrained by the reality,
By people and emotions...

Let your imagination flow
Because that's the "most free"
You can ever be.

Finding my muse in my poetry,
Looking for something...

I don't know how to explain,
But I've felt it strongly.

Struck by inspiration,
At random times...

Such is the beauty...
...of creativeneess

Sometimes calm,
Sometimes chaotic.

The urge
To be productive.

And the peace
Or excitement you feel.

When you're lost,

In a world of your own imagination.

Crave For You

As each day passes by,
I crave for you more & more.

Be it a simple goodmorning text,
Or gifting something of great significance.

You know this and so do I,
We're getting used to each other...

I'm clueless,
Whether it's for the good or bad.

But i find excuses to meet you,
And to stay just a bit longer.

You make my heart race,
And you know it.

You call me sunshine,
And yet you're the one...

Lighting up my world.

A date, i don't want to forget,
A picture, i want to get framed.

A poem, i want to keep reciting,
And a painting full of vibrant colours.

...That i keep looking at,
Just to admire its beauty.

Won't Be Me

One day you'll hold someone's hand,
Who won't be me...

One day you'll end up with a guy,
Who won't be me...

And even though i know it,
It still stings equally

One day you'll be with someone,
Who won't be me.

You won't even recognise my face,
You'll forget all those memories

And those days,
We spent together.

One day you'll be
happier than ever

You want that for yourself
And i wish the same.

Even though it's obvious,
It's still disheartening

One day you'll be

somewhere far away...

And I'll never be able to

call you "mine" again

Home

Always tryna run away,
Now i set you free...

Go reunite with the sky,
For freedom is calling you.

Unlike a pathetic naive fool like me,
You're someone with big dreams.

From above the clouds,
The sun that lights up the word.

Even though the weather
Can be scorching sometimes...

The universe does play favorites,
And you're one of them.

So spread your wings wide,
And don't ever turn back...

The journey can be beautiful,
Without grudges & regret.

I'm not your destination,
But hopefully the last stop before home.

Whenever Our Eyes Meet

Your eyes tell me poems,
Which aren't perfect on paper...

Yet the closest to my heart.

Without any punctuations,
Or rhyming scheme...

A message from your eyes to mine.

Whenever we meet,
It's more like an open mic than a meeting.

Whenever I stare into your eyes,
I feel like reciting a poem...

I know by heart...
But never wrote in the first place.

Butterflies in my stomach?
I feel them from my head to my feet....

Whenever our eyes meet.

Opportunity

An unfamiliar vibe

Out of the world

Unprepared for this

Roller coaster of emotions

I want the best of both worlds

Quite grand yet a peaceful life

With people who care about me

I grew up with no ambitions

But I'm still hoping for happiness

Even though I feel down sometimes,

Even if i lose faith...

I know that I've come this far...

Maybe for a reason

Or maybe just pure luck

Maybe I'll go out like fireworks

Or maybe like a silent voice

Maybe it's pointless

Or maybe it's fate

I know that I'll do something

Even if it's not great

Because I'm born into this world

I won't let my only opportunity slip away.

Reason To Live

What is that you live for?
Please be honest...

Do you have dreams,
Of your own or someone else's...

How much have you sacrificed,
For you aim...

How far do you plan
To play this game...

Lemme rephrase what I said,
What's your reason to live.

Is it because you have
Something to look forward to

Must be nice,
Even if it's hard to stay sane sometimes...

You may even lose hope,
But hold a little longer, have some faith.

It'll be all fine and worth it.

What is that you live for?
Please be honest...

Is it because you have
Someone you love

Someone dear to you,
Who symbolises hope for you.

Through good times and hard times,
Someone who stood by your side.

Must be nice,
Even if it's not sunshine always.

In the end, you'll make it work,
And be happy like you're supposed to be.

What is that you live for?
Please be honest...

Is it something or someone
Or is it just because you're not dead yet...?

Lemme rephrase what I said,
What's your reason to live.

Life can be confusing sometimes,
But at the end of the day...

It's just you,
All by yourself.

Call it meaningful,
Or meaningless...

But you're still...

Thinking and dreaming and
Playing and feeling and
Quiet and screaming...
And just living....

Blue Sky

Blue, blue sky
Reminds me of freedom

As it calls my name,
I simply fly away

Like the wind,
Sometimes soft...

Sometime cold and harsh,
I flow without hesitation.

Kinda warm, kinda cold
Tree shed, leaves green & gold.

I love the blue sky,
And the clouds too...

A scenery that
Soothes my soul

Be it my evening routine,
Or a walk outside.

The blue sky is always
Watching me from above.

2. Akansha Gupta

Akansha Gupta is an ambivert, a budding writer, a dog mom and a self taught dancer.

Besides this, she also likes making mandala art.

Instagram : @akanshaagupta_

Only If

pindrop silence..

just you and me ..

alone..

roaming around the city..

with me sitting on your back ..

hugging you from back..

and my hug getting tighter everytime you stop the bike..

wind blowing on our faces , and beautiful moonlight..

not wanting to leave your side

not wanting to stop hugging you ..

hope we could be like this for ever

the wave of jealousy when someone else comes near you , touches you

and the desire to snatch you away from them , marking you mine and only

mine..

the urge of taking care of you..

wanting to be there for you ..

wanting to listen to your downs..

the urge to be your comfort person..

the urge to be told to your friends as someone who means the world to

you..

day dreaming about how we can spend our lives together..

then a loud thunder occurs and i wake up

realising it was all a dream

a dreamy dream

only if this could be possible in reality

I would be the happiest

One Day

as long as you are present
i feel calm.
as long as i hear your voice
my ears feels glitters.
as long as i see you
my eyes feels warm.
as our eyes meet
my heart can't resist your charm.

your presence is magical.
the thought of you getting subtracted from my life is tragical.
your voice is like a sweet melody
which I'd listen my life if i can wholeheartedly.
your sight is mesmerising
you are always going to be the point of my gazing.
when you look at me while im already looking at you
my heart feels the butterflies i never experienced.

the thought of being with you
holding your hand
looking at your eyes
smiling while maintaining eye contact
admiring your angelic presence
being able to tell you how much i adore you
is something I'd do anything for.
life has to give me chance

one day i will earn it
you are someone i desire
even if I can't have you
never will i stop to admire
you and
everything about you.

It's You

you know those days ? when you don't know yourself

you know those phase? when you don't have your self-esteem.

you know those days? when you cry yourself to sleep

you know those days? when you ask them for attention, validation like a

creep.

you know those days? when nothing makes sense.

yk those days?when you aren't in your proper sense.

it's all in your mind

the solution for all this

that we need to find

we know ourselves better than any possible one.

we know when this all begun

you are the key.

it's just your emotions need to agree.

depression is a part of you

not you

you are tired now

now doesn't last long

YOU are the only thing that lasts long as you last long.

3. Akshi

Akshi likes to write poems in free time. She also has many other hobbies like reading, singing and listening music, observing nature, and being in solitude.

She thinks that our thoughts are a waste if we don't convey them through a medium. So she likes to convey her thoughts by writing poems which gives a beautiful message.

Setting Sun

Walking across the river

Taking small steps

Feeling the wind on my face with a book in my hands

Thinking something unusual

That can't be borne

Taking deep breath to deal with the future ahead

Wiping the tears that are rolling down my cheeks

Then dripping on my shivering hands

Sitting on a bench that was once new

But now got old like my many hopes

Thinking now what to do next

Killing all the hopes inside of starting new

That has once decided to do

Watching the sparkling water with blurry eyes

That's giving me good vibes

Looking at the sun with the shiny face

Yet full of worried look

But it looked like it's smiling with a happy face

Gave it an asking look questioning what do i do

It smiled again like asking me to smile too

Before going away

Then I realized what it wanted me to tell

* It's ok to feel hopeless once but rising again should be your inner voice *

I smiled at it before standing up

Like saying it thanks and goodbye

Be Quiet once

Let's stay silent once
Close your eyes but
Don't let any thoughts come
Stay quiet not because you have got nothing to say
But to see who speaks the most
And to hear everything that you always wanted to
Try to observe who shows off the most
Even after getting little
Stop saying everything that comes up on your tongue
Who knows that may hurt someone
Stay quiet if not sure it's worthy to say or not
But speak if it's a laud
Keep a smile even if not interested in chat but
Don't speak until you know the fact
Show that you can do but dont like to fancy
"Let's don't say"
"Let's don't think"
"Let's just hear"
"Let's be quiet once"

The Night

In the darkest room

Sitting near the window

Looking at the sky

Talking to the few stars visible to me

With a book in my hand

Not wanting to read

Don't know why, but

thinking about something that giving me chills

Words were popping in mind

want my soul to calm

but my heart said

Dear don't hold it, let it go

Asking the universe what's going to be next

Don't know but hoping to be the best

Waiting for something bright like those twinkles

But then realising there is something more brighter than those

Then a glow appeared from behind those heavy clouds

and not me wanting to see it whole,

all stars were looking beautiful until it showed

but now faded from its glow

It glowed like wants to say hii to me

I asked what is the reason of your glow

I am confident within myself he said

Said that I'm not perfect, but

But still glows to hide my flaws

I realised that should shine but

like the moon that even the morning sun can not hide your glow

4. Ankita Negi

Ankita Negi hails from the picturesque town of garhwal.
She loves reading & writing. Besides this, she also loves basketball and firmly believes in self-love.
Instagram : @btw_ankita05

Together Was Our Promise

I woke up broken

Missing how I used to wake up smiling

Knowing that you're already waiting,

Waiting to shower all your love

I don't like crying myself to sleep

I want to feel loved again

I want you to be my side

I want you to come back,

To come back and make love

Together was our promise

I'll come to you soon

Till then

I'll love you from here.

To Be Here With Me

I still search for you in crowd
Looking for you in everyone I meet
I still search for you in every sunrise,
Because you're not here with me
I want you to be here,
To be here with me
But it's too late
You won't come,
You would never.

Without A Goodbye <3

I wish you were here,

I miss how I used to call you mine.

I want to feel your presence again.

For one last time I wish,

We could be together.

For one last time,

I could feel you.

For one Last time,

I could here your voice.

" I'm always here" you promised but you left .

You left,

Without a good bye.

5. Anushree Chauhan

Anushree chauhan is one of the blooming writer among many flowers. She is a nature lover and animal lover. She loves to write poem which gives peaceful and fresh vibes. She is looking forword to give love and peace through her poems. She has worked in many anthologies like Aaksh, flower of light, etc. Her hobbies are singing and sketching but she is interested in almost every things which amuse her and can make her mind engage. She is a linguist, memer, humorous and loves to discover about different culture and traditions. She hopes her poem to be a peaceful sunrise for others.

Instagram : @gg._han

• 48 •

Lost You

I light up the sky with your memories,
I fought with all waves to see marmoris.

I walked through my tears to see you,
But I've fallen, failed to hate you.

It's hard to be yours and I can't be,
So I stopped imagine you and I as we.

I still have your picture in my mind,
Should have tore but independently bind.

Not someone special but I'd love to be a passenger in your life,
I've only wished, waited for your sunrise.

Let's be a stream and follow our own path,
Because there is no reason for me, for you to stay.

It hurts but its okay to left Me in vain,
Just live happily and never mind as I'm used to the rain.

Last Scenery

Your warmth went through my skin to my soul,

The sun witnessed our love till the core,

Blur lenses are unable to capture the moment,

Listen! Hold your love from rolling down,

Its a recall for our last breath's intertwine,

But stay connect to my red string of fate,

Cuz I promised you to be together till after death.

I Mind

Same days, same time,
Long lost so nevermind,
Still eyes and breaking lines,
Heavy life so, major lies,
Cold feet under starry night,
Cracking chirup, shiny eyes,
Smiley mask over dull dry,
Breaking down on soft pile,
Laughing fingers edit my life.

6. Astha Vijay

Astha is an ambivert, potterhead who likes to travel and eat. Always up for deep rejuvenating conversations.

HASYANTRAM.

ALWAYS.

Instagram : @__astha_1903

Paws & Claws

Already missing the one who used to be my euphony
Time passes, days pass, they didn't come

Ever day i waited for them
Sitting in the verandah
Getting radiated from sunbeams

Hoping for them to get well
But wasn't aware that it will take a process
It was the FOURTH day.

The only stress buster for me was them
Thou don't know when life gives you extreme turns

Wasn't a blood relo
But for the first time it was a connection of love

Playing with hankies, poly's and paper's
Was his favourite job

(And an untold story , which you never know)

Still hallucinating .
It was the LAST SECOND DAY ,
Since i felt :
his last breath
his last steps
his paws & claws

his last voice

Surrounding me .

Image

Tears in my eyes,

I can't define

When he goes

I see the same image

which i saw last time.

But this time,

he was white, bonny, weak,

just like the last one.

But he was happy with his brothers, playing dancing & enjoying.

He toh just started his life,

but before he saw the world,

It ended in the blink of an eye.

The joy in his eyes was more than mine.

The calmness he had, i cant describe.

Conjugation

I live the moment, i love the life
I end up every day with a huge smile

My day starts with a yawn
My night ends with dawn

Whenever thee start writing thou never stop
But the nature taught us if we began than we have to end it !

I want to conjugate with the lone pair of my life
'Cause conjugation with lone pair makes you stable

I jumped into the heaven of life
It's just a matter of eyes
You see it as hell and i see it as heaven
Hence, you fell and i swam.

7. Charu Sharma

Charu, a static observer, a melomaniac. Music is like catalyst for her which gives life to Sher hopes. She seeks freedom, positivity and happiness.

Not Yours

My ecstacy is bounded,

Your presence is not anymore surrounded.

My life is caged behind the bars,

Impotently, fighting wars after wars.

I'm tryna exhale this pain,

You said you are done but what if I'm not, what if for you I'm still insane.

This whole journey strikes me as being dilapidated,

Each time you made me felt like I'm the one who is underrated.

I'm no more me now,

This skeleton is managing to breathe somehow.

Didn't you said that you will be always mine?

Then why did you left me alone here for dyin'?

My fuckin' living has become a game of paradox,

As our love is no more on the rocks.

Feelings have become inaccessible for my heart now,

Also the brain lost the capacity to answer- What, When and How!

This dark, dismal night is appreciating my fear,

And that agony which I can never bear.

This lonely isolated room is as downhearted and blue as me,

Not that charming like before as it used to be.

The leaves are being wilted from the tree,

And so the strength from me.

You were the only saviour of my badtimes,

The leading irreplaceable part of my love rhymes.

Slowly, even the moon is loosing the glow,

So the river it's flow.

Tears are just rolling and rolling down,

Except you why everyone seems to be a stranger in this town?

Obsessed

Precious was Your Presence,

Ardour was Your Touch,

Toxic was Your Love,

And eventually Lie became US.

Hypocrite is You,

But now Shattered, devastated and alone is only me

8. Drishti Singhal

She is Drishti Singhal. She loves to read and write. She also has hobbies like Dancing and singing. She has also worked in many anthologies like Hedging your bets; Unsung tales; Shine of love..etc
Instagram : @_drishti.ii_

Memories

That day snowfall started..
I was already late!
I was walking through empty streets..
Dude! It was my first blind date!!

I reached cafe ASAP..
The cafe was closed!
It ruined my mood..
And my mind got Frosed!!

Suddenly a boy came from behind..
He was cute enough to melt my heart!
I already thought my future with him..
And decided to never get apart!!

By moving out from my thoughts, have seen him again..
WTH! Hw was that guy only with whom I have planned to move out
today!
I smiled gently and felt sorry for being late..
Being ok he smiled too and his smile just made my day!!

After 2 minutes of awkward silence..
He told me of all the arrangements he did!
Oh my God a surprise..
I got so excited like a kid!!

He took me to the cafe.. All rights were dim!
After knowing each other..
I felt in love with him!!

Now your photo on a wall with a garland..
Everyday reminds me of you!
Maybe God doesn't want us to be together..
But I can't give your place to anybody in my heart!!
I will only love you forever and ever!!!

Raindrops

I am in love with these raindrops..
Which creates a beautiful view!
When I stands under the rain..
It made me reminds of you!!

Few years ago, when you had left me alone..
I cried in this rain!
That rain had hide my tears..
But it cant hide my pain!!

I have forgot you..
And your memories aldo gone!
But whenever i come in the rain..
I feel like i am alone!!

I Don't Know

I don't know

Why i cry at night!!

Why I am unable to fight!!

I don't know

What to do in future!!

Why I dont nurture!!

I don't know

Why I have become selfish!!

Why but I feel like this is my finish!!

I don't know

Why god has planned for me!!

But I think only love can save me!!

9. Khushi Gulwani

Khushi Gulwani is very fond of Spending time with nature and observing things .

While observing things she love to write with full of emotions.

Besides writing she love to Listen music . She always try to follow her heart in this beautiful world.

Instagram: _khushi_gulwani

Memories

Lying under the sky
Reliving the memory in front of my eyes
Painful are the goodbyes
That make my heart cries

Not knowing it's the last day
With whom I use to spend the whole day

Crying for hours in dark and daylight
With whom I saw my future bright
Wipe it coz the pain will whine
And showed my beautiful smile

Live the moment fully
Until it becomes memory
Once it become memory,
eyes will get teary
Don't let it go coz then it will be scary

Taking a deep breath
With the closing eyes
Moving in life
With a painful smile
And missing a part of my life

Life is full of smiles, tears and memories
Smile fades

Tears dries

But forever stays are memories

Selenophile

In the hours of darkness,
All alone
Over analyzing my past 24 hours
My mind explode,
Not wanna think anymore

Need some calmness ,
To end this mind mess
Went near the open casement,
Looked at the sleeping planet

All darkness at Night,
With the full moon bright

Felt like
Night is telling me some line
Tried to realize
Moon is telling me to shine
Even in hardships of mine

My soul said,
You are the best
Among the rest
In millions of stars
You are the brightest

My heart smiled,

All brain thoughts cleared.

New hope arrive

And made me SELENOPHILE

Precious Life

Let's be ourself,
Which sparkle the soul of oneself.

Love yourself,
But don't be self obsessed.

Live life,
Don't stab knife.

Dig into your life,
To know yourself more .

Celebrate every victory,
Because life is a mystery.

Don't wait for the moment ,
Make all moment yours.

Life is unpredictable ,
Wanna live more .

Play the games of life,
With the eyes full of shine.

10. Mumal S.

A day dreamer penning down her random thoughts and unheard stories , giving an insight of her own world

Email : mumals1130@gmail.com

Lonely Stars

I still search for you
among these faces
in those empty corridors
and those isolated stairs

In busy lights
and passing cars
on windy nights
and lonely stars

It's been long since
I called you mine
but the time has passed
for you and I

But I am trying to live without you..
holding onto these prettyy scars
and lonely stars...

For You

I look for you...

in the sun ;
the moon ,

the sounds of rain ;
the flows of wind ,

the rustling of leaves ;
the sunlight that beams ,

In all those small things
that we cherished ;
I still look for you...

I look for..
the shine in your eyes ;
the glow on your face ;
the melody of your laughter ;
I still look for you...

They still come to me ...
As fresh as the spring ;
it comes to me ;
make my heart flutter ;
and make me ;
look for you...

Beginning

Remember
the strangers that met ;
the effect it had ;

The corner seat ;
One beach for two ;

with those little sparkling eyes
looking at me ;

Stirring my thoughts ;
making it hazy ;

It gives me goosebumps ;
can't lie ;
Because it was the beginning ;
of YOU and I ,

The tingles i felt when
you spoke my name ;

The electricity that bolted in me ;
when u sat next to me ;
and our hands brushed againt each other ;

Wish we could go back ;
relive those moments ;
and intertwine our hands ;

and say that it was always ;

You and I...

11. Priyansh Bagga

Priyansh Bagga is an ambivert who likes to write, click pictures and hit the gym.

Instagram : @_priyansh.11

Rooftop

I laid on the roof top
Under the dark sky,
Staring at the stars
And wondering that who will
Be my forthcoming consort

And pondering that she
must be thinking bout me

Also,
Will this feeling will come in my
Nightmare.
Or not...

I want that in my dreams.

Nightmare

A short film,
Yes dude, that's my dream

Love, suspense, horror
Or thriller
Either the detective, or the killer

Neither profit nor loss;
In my fantacy,
Where I am the only boss

A desire that I don't
Want to end

I love that feeling,
Someone is healing
Someone is stealing
And bro, I am
Dealing with my Dreaming

Mask

Wear it! Wear it! Wear it!
Where are you going?
You are not the GOD
What are you doing?

Look at your grandma,
She is sewing...

2, 4, 6, 8, ten
She never gets tired
While makin 'em
Wear it! My dear Ben

The pandemic is not
Over yet...
It is a part of your
Closet!

Some are plain,
Some are colourful.
And that printed goose,
Which will you choose?
I like that N-Ninety Five
Gimme a High Five

It has become the fashion now
If you know you know...

12. Sakshi Sharma

An extroverted introvert who writes when she can't sleep! Pursuing English(H) from Delhi University, this talents believes that We are just stories at the end so let's write before life finishes its chapter. Instagram : @sac.sheee

Peep Into Me

Giving you chances were actually addition to my hopes

that may be it will be better than yesterday and Best for tomorrow

I tried my fuckin best to save the essence present in our bond

and you tried your best to ask for more chances if it could

I kept on showering those chances upon you as they were kind of worthless

and you kept on destroying with so much initiative as they were kind of

rootless

From: "It will take time to understand how to live with you and for

you..with me"

To: "It will take time to understand you don't need me and so I should be"

Have you ever tried to peep into me and See- (a)How much I wanted and

how much you brought?

(b)How much I loved and how much I got?

(c)How much I tried and how much I expected?

(d)How much I showed and how much you accepted?

WELL it will remain between you and me that I loved and love you like

hell and It will remain with me..only me that I pushed my limits to get u

back from my already broken heart.

13. Sanskriti Saumya

A passionate singer rising from the land of forests, Jharkhand
Who is still a high school student and is working to shed lights on sensitive or unheard topics through writing.
Instagram:- @Sanskritisaumya_

Twitter:- @Sanxriti1

Empty

What is this empty feeling
I feel so dark and hollow
I can hear my heart sinking again
My saliva is hard for me to swallow

Everything is going fine
Then why am I numb again
I keep walking down to the broken paths
Of my memory lane

This isn't what I wished for
Its like a curse upon my brain
Its like my feelings are dying
And maybe I won't feel again

I cry so hard and hard
That I choke on my breath
I try my best to calm me down
But everytime I break

My mind is all blank now
But still its full of stress
The overwhelming feel of hollowness
Maybe this is emptiness....

Addiction

What day is it again?
Because I don't remember
Its middle of the june
But its cold like december

My body is fidgeting
But my mind can't move
Its like the same things
Are playing on a loop

As i'm getting sober
I reach for it again
Its just a tiny pill
But makes me forget all the pain

The struggles of reality
Are too much to handle
I prefer my slowed down world
Where no one's vulnareble

They say if I keep this up
I'm soon gonna die
The amount of times life fucked me up
Honestly I don't wanna stay alive...

Persona

I have a cheeky smile
While hiding all that trauma
Believing that one day
They will all be punished by the karma

Being all extroverted and happy
Is one of my traits
But have they ever wondered
If any of this was fake

That physically average girl
Who's always full of life
Is she actually that that happy?
Or just living a lie

She's got nothing to stress about
I wish I was like her
But no one's ever known
That she had always lived in fear

Oof! That girl's so full of herself
She always creates the drama
But you've never known her for a second
You've just known her Persona....

Trust

In this crowd of fakeness
Where love is only lust
Where machines are oiled everyday
But human hearts are taking rust

Don't fall for the mirage on faces
It will eat you from inside
And if you get swallowed in it
You won't have any place to hide

I've gathered all shatters of mine
And made it into a pile
I know i won't ever laugh again
But i will always keep a smile

I will give them every inch of my heart
But don't u mistake that for my trust
Because everything can be smushed and mended
But not your broken Trust.

Toxic Love

All of your "hey goodmorning love"
Turned into "why do you mess up"
Am I in love or am I just stuck?!
You said finding you was best of my luck

I've been trying to prove my love for long enough
Your complimets now sounded like mock
You made me feel like you were always above
Playing the victim you said I was tough?!

Cheating with other girls pushing me down
Took me in as your queen and then threw off my crown
You used to smile at me now you always frown
Stabbed me with knife like words until I fell on the ground

I should only wear things that you would allow
Don't meet up with guys since they are bad crowd
You came drunk and hit me, threw me out of house
I should've felt sad but I felt free from your toxic love

14. Satyam Kumar Choudhary

A teenager hailing from the land of five rivers, Punjab
Who has completed his high school and now looking forward to make
a career out of Writing.
Instagram?: satyamchaudhary22
Snapchat?: satyam271103
Twitter?: Satyamchy1

Young Hearts

We are young hearts looking for an old fashioned kind of love

Our mind follow the new trends and our heart still has expectations that someone could love as those in the movies of 60's

We're not stable, life is running at its fastest pace but still we want a stable relationship with someone with whom we can make our life stable

We're just those old fashioned boys in their teenage or in their 20's who are wearing the mask of this new generation...!!

Perfection

You know sometimes we pick the perfect vase and the perfect flowers from somewhere and just put them together.

They are beautiful but not look as good as we expected.

Both the vase and the flowers are perfect but not perfect for each other.

They may have their less perfect counterparts somewhere in the world waiting for them so that they could look perfect together.

Perfection has nothing to do with the individuality, if two imperfect souls make a perfect pair, that's the most beautiful and perfect thing in the holy universe.

Reality

The ones who act broken are actually not

But the ones you never think, are broken as hell but they keep on smiling as they know noone really cares

If you tell anyone that you're broken they'll reply they are even broken and in more worse condition than you

But you know what smiling brings us?

It brings the self confidence that we can fight any situation with a smiling face and a cheerful mindset

I know I'm low right now but I also know this is not my place

I know I won't meant to be there

I'm here to touch the skies of glory, I'm here to just cut down all the burdens and fly high

I'm here to live a life of my desires, I'm here to life a life of my choice

If you stop me from being me, I'll just dump you

It's that simple...!!

15. Vishesh Singh Bhadauria

Vishesh Singh Bhadauria is a budding writer who's also passionate about gaming and wishes to represent India on a global platform. He wants to inspire everyone and make his parents proud

Instagram : @carnival_writeups

Her Smile

After being trapped by those eyes,
The other does of pleasure was her smile.

Just by smiling a single time,
She took away all the pain and grief from my mind.

Looking at her smile made me freez,
She gave me a moment of love and peace.

She became a godess of beauty just by a single smile,
Whom I could worship my entire life.

I would sacrifice my own life,
If it was to protect her smile.

I was fooling myself my whole life,
But now i know that all i ever wanted was her smile.

Unfair Life

No matter which path I tried,
The result was meant to be declared by unfair life.

Ignoring my feelings and putting them aside,
She chose a rich and better guy.

I just wanted to hear it once,
That they were proud of their son.

I wanted to stand out as someone great,
But this life proved that i was just an ordinary remake.

Healing all the pain with a glass of wine,
I had no option but to continue this unfair life.

Her Warmness

My soul dying out screaming for peace,
Growing a cruel demon inside.

Almost about to release my anger,
Until I see your face.

Your charming smile,
Softening my heart.

Clinging to your warmness,
Taking your remedy of love.

Leaves me with a single phrase,
Darling, I'm home ?

Previous Works By The Author (compiler)

• Published as an Author (solo) of the book 'The Fading Bud' (ISBN : 9781639202218) 10th May, 2021

• Published as an Author (solo) of the book 'The Evanescent Floret' (ISBN : 9781685236533) 11th August, 2021

• Published as an Author (solo) of the book 'The Dwindling Bloom' (ISBN : 9781685869939) 18th October, 2021

• Published as a compiler of the book 'Flame Petals' (ISBN : 9798885469609) 30th December, 2021

• Published as a compiler of the book 'Kavya Pankhudi' (ISBN : 9798885698719) 27th January, 2022

• Published as an Author (solo) of the book 'Warbling In The Wind' (ISBN : 9798885912266) 1st February, 2022

THE
FADING
BUD
Suryansh S. Chauhan

The Evanescent Floret
Suryansh S. Chauhan

The
Dwindling
Bloom
Suryansh S. Chauhan

Flame
Petals
Compiled by
Suryansh S. Chauhan

काव्य पंखुड़ी
कविता संग्रह
सूर्यांश एस. चौहान
(द्वारा कंपाईल्ड)

Warbling In The Wind
Suryansh S. Chauhan

THANKYOU FOR READING!

www.ingramcontent.com/pod-product-compliance
Lightning Source LLC
Chambersburg PA
CBHW021451150726
47989CB00001B/495